Lyric Pieces for the Young
for Piano
by Norman Dello Joio

Contents

T0051118

EDWARD B. MARKS MUSIC COMPANY

EXCLUSIVELY DISTRIBUTED BY

HAL•LEONARD® CORPORATION

7777 W. BLUEMOUND RD. P.O. BOX 13819 MILWAUKEE, WI 53213

Lyric Pieces for the Young

Total duration: 14 min., 10 sec.

NORMAN DELLO JOIO

1. Boat Song

Duration: 2 min., 20 sec.

4

2. Prayer of the Matador

Duration: 2 min.

3. Street Cries

Duration: 1 min.,45 sec.

4. Night Song

cresc. poco a poco

legato sempre

Duration: **3 min.,40 sec.**

5. The Village Church

Duration: 2 min., 15 sec.

6. Russian Dancer

Duration: 2 min, 10 sec.